A
Sentimental
Hairpin

Flower Conroy

Tolsun Books
Flagstaff, Arizona

Be first and be lonely.

Ginni Rometty

Table of Contents

1. Blue o'clock in the Morning
3. The Phenomenology of Spirit-Conjuring
5. Static
6. Lesser Known Facts About the Moon
7. [at midnight Split]
8. Some Scratch About Aesthetics
10. [You promised to say nothing]
11. Love in the Form of Bleach
13. Graveyard Squall
14. [leaning into the pleasant]
15. Before Diagnosis
16. Fourth Floor Ward
17. [it's too late]
19. Aesth. Scratch, Cont.
22. Ipse Dixit
24. [I surprised her troubled voice]
25. Love in the Form of Hush & Seep
27. Godiva's Glove
28. [bed, lock the hall door behind me]
29. Decapitation
30. [to be Obedient]
31. An Outline of a Theory of Accident
34. Love in the Form of Psithurism
36. [hurt, —remembering]
37. Love in the Form of QVC Binge
39. Mercy, for the Connoisseur of Sugar
40. Elegy for the Dodo
41. How Many Fingers Am I Holding Up?
48. [quiet. I should be thought; I'd]
50. Love in the Form of "Nip," "Smidgen," "Pinch," & "Dash"

Table of Contents Cont.

51. Last Supper

52. [a picture of the evening]

54. Do not pity the deer,

55. [heart]

56. Harlequin Punch & Spider Corn Bread

59. Poem Primarily About Moss

60. [I explained the peculiar]

61. The Disintegration of Annie

62. Love in the Form of Far-Offness

64. Twyndyllyngs

65. ["Yes," I said, glancing at my wrist]

66. Conjurer

67. [Problems, problems, in every direction: what]

68. Elegy of the Tigerwolf

69. [relax]

71. Love in the Form of Rock-a-Bye Baby

73. What the Scapegoat Whispered

74. Sound curls in the tunnel of my ear

76. [the doorway of]

77. Fish in the Bougainvillea

79. [I burrowing weeping]

80. Recap in Nonlinear Time

82. [...alone in the world... wake]

84. What Happened to Nancy?

87. [but in the end,]

88. Doppler

89. [be mutton]

90. In a Roman Plaza

92. Love in the Form of Shell Shock

94. Geolocation

96. Love in the Form of Medium (as Vessel)

Table of Contents Cont.

97. [I left, never dreaming]
99. Because to Dress Means to Eviscerate
101. [I entirely real, and]
102. Ministry
103. ars poetica apologia
110. Love in the Form of Flowers Drowning Flowers
111. [unconnected]
112. Erasure Erasure
116. Collect Call from Outer Space—Do You Accept the Charges?
119. Acknowledgements

A Sentimental Hairpin

But no, her words are in orbit

while I move shamefully forward,

the guardian of lost things

Mary Ruefle

Blue o'clock in the Morning

Of the dog found
in the cold, in a cage
in the river?
Sometimes the quality
of mercy is not
strained, it drop-
peth as the gentle rain[1],
& sometimes it descends
like an axe blade. Hadn't I
considered the act
of smothering an offering,
dignity & *quality*
of life being
how we talked
those nights around
the coma?
Sometimes I imagine
like that myth-
ological deity mid-
change, part feather-
dimension, part-fingerprint,
I am a humxn-swan,
conic face, eyes wet
with space & muted
reach. Of course I was
making the mistake
of looking with-
out & not within.
There is beauty

in silence & there is silence
in beauty & you can find
both in a bicycle[2]
but there's no reconciling
the one millionth of one
1,000,000th of a second
difference between. I said *swan*
but I think I mean
egret. Or cormorant.
It's the neck. Dipping
into others' lakes,
dripping others' waters.
I'd choose cruelty
for the cruel
but an eye is never
an eye, a hand never just
a hand.
One can still hear hell
in shelter. If you be
the river I'll be the mutt.
If you be the cold
       I'll be a hull, holding

---

[1] *Shakespeare*
[2] *Bamboozle on Pinterest*

The Phenomenology of Spirit-Conjuring[1]

Is snake's opposite airfoil or killdeer
or other?

None can run from Gäd
& in my side-eye,

a glitch of flight
when a bird scythes

(this being their migratory season)
past the sun-

room's bride-glass windows.
Enveloped in leaves, pupil

brassy as a tack, millipede
clamped in its beak,

in those micro-
moments, I'm knifed

with heartsickness
until, in montage,

the grackle reveals itself.
So much doesn't exist

when one can't
remember. Like touch, after.

---

[1]Phrase taken out of context from Daniel Schulke's *Veneficium*

Static

In the oil-on-canvas
painting, "Flood," a half-
dressed gamine extends
a leg over a roadside railing
into encroaching mist
but I cannot tell
if these are the hours
just before or after
the freshet. If I
imagine you clicking
keys, picking through shells
say, along a bay where the cliffs
sometimes cave, spilling
teeth, does the theory of simultaneity
mean you're also listening to beach
fossils & wild nothing in a room
without furniture, chattering
10 million years ago
through the greendark? My mind
pearls. Sand spilled on black velvet.
And so electric
eels swim the radio whalefall
between exchanges. Vines talking
to themselves. Pouring
river into river, you were becoming more
& more, the shore's wind-carved
        equations.

Lesser Known Facts About the Moon

"She's a bit free with her 'we'."
Joe Ahearn about Dorianne Lux's poem
"Facts About the Moon"

We were: ugly, gleaming
our reflected semblance in a well
of unpotable water
the stones held their cold against. We were touched
by the Old One. Our ultimate talent:
striptease. However, without precision,
concision's nothing. Each day waxes a soupçon
of a second longer
than the one it follows; mean-
while We were: avenues of lathes, lace-
wings littering labyrinth halls, a corridor of high-
balls at noon. You'd think knowing We all'll
die is some constellation. Consultation. Con-
sideration. But We were: either in the business
of making meaning or making feeling. Raked
fore & aft, We were: cut-
throat, throwing the hammer, We were: Icarus'
mistress, & We were: idiosyncratic as a switchback
in the distance.
Tidal locking rock. Addiction given up
too late. The razor-
clam shucked clean.
Just because you've never heard Us speak
doesn't mean We're silent. What you call *blood*
is just rust-colored shadowing.

[at midnight Split]

at midnight Split

into

dream—I forgot

private, private
tension, and the hour,

I'm incognito,
some film

or

vague

almost

,   so oft   in lve

at midnight Split/ into dream—I forgot/ you're the one/ with languages private,
private/ tension and the hour/ I'm incognito, some film/ or vague almost/ so oft/ in lve

Some Scratch About Aesthetics

Someone once offered me
the following feed-
back: *You are letting the syntax*
slow you down. Syntax
should be used, rather, to speed one up;
& *This feels like a closing-down*
when this poem s. b. opening up @
the end. But should there not be
something said for stilling, sitting
statuesque for untold, un-
interrupted hours on a bench, drinking-
in a piece of artwork until
like a dandelion time-
elapsing into wishhead, strata
by strata, inbeing
unfolds into subtexture—
& what was an exchange
of data becomes experience itself, a pause
amplified, magnified ambergris
among sand & gravel? Yes,
the most common language
is body; the world presses
in aura & rebus, disappears
the fringe, & what gives
pattern matter *is* its fracturing.
And though they ought
instigate a quickening
below the surface—
sentences needn't rush.

This morning after breakfast
of cubed melon
drizzled in lemon, I misread
Touching Harms the Art
as *Touching Arms
the Heart*. When it comes to instant
gratification & Boschian delights, I strive
as long as possible—& not
one nanosecond longer—to stave
       off ecstasy. Then I eat the whale,
       bite by bite.

[You promised to say nothing]

You promised to say nothing
                    since no lasting harm

.

The   horse was   close to

fresh
        time   cleared the hedge, but still needing a
                                field.
                unnerved—reared and threw
                                        first
                                        wood

        you   returned to her needle-
    and so, you think perhaps you may yet come
to joy sic
                                                I
mourned, searching for a strand of   color,
        I   must
abandon what gives — you—   pleasure.
There has to be reciprocity

        night   was flanked by thin-silvered
tongue

You promised to say nothing since no lasting harm. / The horse was close to fresh. /
time cleared the hedge, but still/ needing a field. / unnerved—reared and threw first
wood/ you returned to her needle-/and so, you think perhaps/ you may yet come to
joy sic/ I mourned, searching for a strand of color, / I must abandon what gives—
you—pleasure. / There has to be reciprocity/ night flanked by thin-silvered tongue

Love in the Form of Bleach

The broom handle's rubbed the skin raw
        between my thenar webspace, sweeping
& re-sweeping my mother's floors.
        And while I try to be full of grace

when stoned, it was like ballet
        dancing through muddy water
yesterday, smashing into corners
        & stubbing along the dense

carpet, navigating the vacuum. In the ICU
        my mother keeps taking without
adding when I try to (re)teach her Scopa[1].
        And though we are laughing—her more

so—giddy even—about her backwards
        math of snatching a seven & a six with a one
I'm freaking. Fanning her head, she says
        after a pause, *I still have diminishing*—.

On the video chat the doctor instructs she lift
        her arms. Then: *Hold them out, like carrying*
a pizza box. Now close your eyes.
        When she shuts her eyes she lets fall

her arms. Because she's hard
        of hearing, the nurse & I encourage her
to again hold the make-believe box,
        Now close your eyes. She cups her hands

to her face as if covering her nose
        & cheeks with invisible cheese.
When we finally get her to extend
        her arms *while* shutting her eyes: *See*

how the right arm hovers lower? She wants
        to come home; take a shower; sit in a chair.
I need another day or two.
        My laboring's only just beginning.

---

1 *Italian card game; "Scopa" translates into "To Sweep," as in, to sweep all the cards from the table but also is a euphuism for "to fuck," as in, to fuck(over) your neighboring player*

Graveyard Squall

       Ash Branch Church
Road. Rice & ice cubes
for lunch
the next day
because I was hungover.
The night blushed
before strolling among the tufts
of Spanish moss clotting
the oak boughs. Stone slabs
whose names & dates
precipitation & wind've
near-erased. Sky cleaved.
Ecstasy, apostasy. There was no
returning whence,
no finding shelter
in the gushing damning weather.
Socks dampened. Squelching
between worlds, among
the long dead in their worm
garden, it seemed
a cleansing, the warm
parish rain. Such that,
much after, when we returned
to the hotel
the lobby chilled us
as if it were a root
cellar & we were spider
eyes spiking dark.

[leaning into the pleasant]

leaning into the   pleasant

   I'm not sure where I left the glasses

   my arm in   the sun

   Perforce, I let him lead me back to   stable ,

                                   I

   reached the yard,   damp with
                       gaze.

                I look   the poor
beast and thought   wickedly
must have been *born* old enough to father the uni‐
verse.

   Behind me,   ingratiating. This
is a private assignation,

        I circled

taking a   glance about. A wooden door stood

leaning into the pleasant/ I'm not sure where I left the glasses/ my arm in the sun/ Perforce, I let him/ lead me back to stable, / I reached the yard, damp/ with gaze. I look the poor beast/ and thought wickedly: he must have been born old/ enough to father the universe. / Behind me, in‐gratiating. This is a private assignation. / I circled/ taking a glance about. A wooden door stood

Before Diagnosis

Ghost pipe knuckling out
of the dirt beside the wild asparagus.
Like the scrying of a fortune teller, a grackle's head
rises in the gazing ball's galactic glass,
yellow eye magnified, exaggerated beak.
Half-folding a shirt before allowing it to crumple
into the basket at my feet.
To breathe the honeysuckled oxygen
of this childhood yard, a Tuesday afternoon in late
August. Or is today Wednesday
on another planet? The sky darkens. Threatens
to anvil strike, to set a roof on fire.
Then does.

Fourth Floor Ward

A paper cup of pills later—. Scaffolding, proboscis, wire, beak.
There's a beauty-mark of water obfuscating the ceiling tile

& on the sill a fly hollows; small perforations sieve the sheets.
I imagine receiving divine instruction akin to grass interpreting

sky. Air blowing into the eyes. Cold fusion. Sun shower.
Through the Cyclopic view of the kaleidoscope, the trees

tear out their leaf-hair. With another crank they exasperate
green fistfuls into their barked mouths. In a patch of afternoon

light beside the fountain—I spied a blue cat turn into a god.
The cat was not blue but *blue.*

[it's too late]

it's too late—perhaps

night

snorted

birth , is it   present, wicked

one?   suddenly sober, "I *think*

— I *feel*

a slip,"

to   : open   —and

be chosen   you

beam   expansively

"A   fly

underfoot

only want to see   star orders.

arose

doesn't need to see   star orders;

along

my hand warmly,   a

real pleasure.   you

cut   smoothly,   I

insist   never forgive me for not

bringing   eyes

it's too late—perhaps./ night snorted birth, is it present, wicked one?/ suddenly sober, "I think—I feel/ a slip,"/ to: open—and be chosen/ you beam expansively/ "A fly underfoot and I/ only want to see star orders./ arose doesn't need to see star orders;/ along my hand warmly,/ a real pleasure. you/ cut smoothly,/ insist / never forgive me for not bringing eyes

Aesth. Scratch, Cont.

What are we thinking? What are we telling ourselves,
and where does this inner voice come from?

from Look Into My Eyes: How to
Hypnotize Anyone

Drama's inherent in the form.
Or it fails to be.

When R said, *You're my favorite tart,*
it was the sweetest thing she'd ever
muttered to me so I knew it was
a compliment to be taken
with a shot of tequila to the heart.

It's not what you say but how
you Gerard-Manley-Hopkins it: the dove
dove a bow
to bow & arrow.

If it's not content,
then it's tone. If it's not con-
tent, then it's sad
if not downright lamentable.

The ox-
cart hitched before the ox? Con-
text.

Like a dust-
cloaked cuckoo clock

in the basement cawing
its thirteen *evermores,* tex-
ture accrues
below surface
but it's image that's haruspex.

When asked what he missed
most on his 200-day
space tour, the astronaut answered
not "Sex,"
but: "Bird chirps & cafe noises."

Still vexing, however
is: is a bathtub a bathtub
on Mars?[1]

The way any log is haunted by the woods
it once was.

Are not (at least in writing) questions
oft rhetorical & heightened elocution
self-executing, ala cocktail of Molotov?

How do you know you're not already hypno-
tized?! interro-
banged the palm reader.

Keep the key skeletal, the map a fragment
& the door ajar with a jar
of pennies: i.e. compose for the retina
but hone for the ~~cochlea~~ inner ear.

There're abandoned ghost-
nets that, fait victorious,
agog,
insatiable, continue to trap
lobster & fish.
Anchored
yet adrift,
crates lopsided with gill & claws scissoring.

O, suffering's
like air
but syntax's levitation.

Don't
(try to)
explain away
mystery.

To extract emotion, to exact the abstract?
Drop
        your goddamn grief into a bucket.

---

[1] From Stephen Dobyns' *Best Words, Best Order,* "there is an old conundrum that asks is a bath-
tub a bathtub on Mars? Implied by this is the idea that something is defined by its function."

Ipse Dixit[1]

The fold equivalent
To the thought. Climbing
The ladder, & mastering
Vaguery is how I began to think
Of my friend with
The bright hair, & not without
A dash of bitters
In the drink. It's not jealousy
As much as it is a sadness
For her & the love-
Liest of emptinesses she calls:
Loneliness. A terrible sadness
For myself. A house
On the water. A house on the water
In the rain. A copper chain
Hung from the eaves to lead—to *drive*
The braided earthbound sky river
Downward. Sometimes it's as if my
Heart's a comet caught inside a hummingbird
But I'm immobilized, in the kitchen, hand
Gripping the counter-edge, floaters
Jellyfishing my vision.
When I see her again I'll tell her how
I've missed her, I'll hold
Her against me, as a friend does,
I'll ask how she's been.
And if she reveals
Some dark secret, some blue
Feather, I'll breathe

Nothing of it. Shadowy
Structure. Bird
Nest or paper cave. I'll keep
My damn mouth shut.

---

[1] An arbitrary or dogmatic statement

[I surprised her troubled voice]

I   surprised   her troubled voice.
                                             fain
                    know   I
                              must
              sacrifice you   darling

                         like
money,

              though
difficult,   I
          won't matter—   less
                              in my part of the
house.
                                        I mean
you would

                                   leave
         like
           a wing
                                              I haven't
come to the end of where I know I can go.

              I could still have babies

I surprised her troubled voice. / fain/ know I must sacrifice you darling/ like money, / though difficult, I won't matter—/ less in my part of the house. / I mean/ you would leave like a wing/ I haven't come to the end of where/ I know I can go. / I could still have babies

Love in the Form of Hush & Seep

My mother repeats she suffered
No permanent damage,
says, *I'm good. I'm good. No*

permanent damage. Then
ventures outside to smoke
an imaginary cigarette. Which is

really just residual habit:
her sitting on the back porch
looking into her phone

or staring into a book. I get that lost
look too, woolgathering through
the mundane. How, because it's against

the basement cinderblock (& I was stoned)
the dryer seemed permeating, space-
ship-like as I scraped out the chamber

where the lint caught: tiny mown field
of gray cloud-down, or meadow of Queen
Anne's lace cobwebbed in a cat's cradle

of trajectories of silk a sudden snow
unspools upon. Thus blanketing it.
Or is it blanking it? A—what do you call

those specialized tools for combing fleece,
brushes you rake against one another,
the sheepknot between thus being undone

into strands? I feel like that. Grappling
with where my mother's mind is, I
feel raked thin. When I asked my mother

about the faucet left still running
after she exited the rehab bathroom,
                despite my eavesdropping

the water cascading down the drain,
        she answered *No. I shut it off.*

Godiva's Glove

Dragging soft along my innermost
cheek: nail edges. Knuckles, glimpse of wrist;
the palmate form *shaping* me. Kidskin & stitch, I keep for myself
the lifeline's orange peel scent, its bareback dampness.
I've touched the skeleton

of an umbrella blown to origami
by a sudden blustering. I've turned on
the lamp, turned off the lamp of a room someone smoked quietly
in the dark of. And I've fallen in slush into the gutter
& lay there, the whole gluttonous sky above me exposed.

[bed, lock the hall door behind me]

bed, lock   the hall door behind me

something was afoot.   There was no
question
                        How many times   waited
the fire   ? In sleep, the lovely face was
infinitely sad.   light   disarranging the
blanket, one hand
chilly when I touched it.

her fingers curled

            I knelt down, murmuring,
                                    She sighed
deeply   into the corner
                                    I tried
to withdraw. There was nothing   but
                        the floor
      I   anguished   .
   what made her dangerous—

   alive

bed, lock/ the hall door behind me/ something was afoot/ There was no question/ How many times waited the fire? / In sleep, the lovely face was infinitely sad. / light disarranging the blanket, one hand/ chilly when I touched it. / her fingers curled/ I knelt down, murmuring, / She sighed deeply into/ the corner/ I tried to withdraw. There was nothing/ but the floor/ I anguished. / what made her/ dangerous alive

Decapitation

I cut your face
out of all the photos.
Not to ex-
scind you
but in attempt
to see
your absence. To see
what I look like from
the outside without.
I peeped
through each hole
to absorb
what your vacancy
gazed. The walls
were the walls,
the television,
the television. Unchanged
in its flux, the lava
lamp was the same globular
bubbling neon lava
lamp. At my feet, scissors
amidst the confetti
of decollated heads,
all yours, staring up at me.

[to be Obedient]

to be   Obedient
found   under a
weeping willow.
            wait   he's cut himself

            there's   nunrest
        an upset; he's digging into these

                                    years

He went pale green at the gills while I related the
inner staircase,   the search of my room,

                        letters in my evening
bag,

                        a mystery—
                        I outlined the
theory of accident

to be Obedient/ found under a weeping willow. / wait/ he's cut himself/ there's unrest/ an
upset;/ he's digging into these years/ He went pale green at the gills while I related/ the inner
staircase, the search/ of my room, / letters in my evening/ bag, a mystery—I outlined the
theory/ of accident

An Outline of a Theory of Accident

Our linear concept of time means nothing
to nature. —Robert Lanza

I. *Flashback Hallucinosis*
    A. Presage of Heimlich
        1. I *hadn't* realized the vision was pre-
        monition until two days later
            a. when I found myself trying
            b. to speak with jazz hands
            c. gagging at the kitchen sink
        2. The most unnerving part wasn't
            a. the watching of oneself from above
            b. the watching of oneself from behind
            c. staring into the drain
            d. nor the dreamy reminiscent feeling of
              asphyxiating
        3. but that whom I daydreamed saved me
            a. saved me
    B. What is it they say about foresight being all acuity?
        1. It's my head which feels
            a. ghastly
            b. like a pitcher of milk
               1. on the railing
              2. in the fog
              3. some spider octogonally spins
                 the surface of
        2. Written in the codes in blood, in the helixes
            a. When I smear the mirror with red
                1. nothing dramatic, just a cut
                 fingertip
                2. harrow, oracle, streak

   b. it is to see myself as if skimming under
    a lake's surface

II. *Flashback Eventual*
  A. Morning I return D's missed call
    1. *Skinny hung herself*
      a. monkey gripped her by the back
       of her neck
      b. her wrists
      c. her small tits
    2. She battled the spike
    3. Fought—sweet Jesus—moonrock
    4. the witch & the beast
    5. I hadn't spoken to her in 15 years at least
    6. *Job axed her*
    7. *Boyfriend left for smokes, never came back*
    8. Survived
      a. by a son she lost
      b. custody of
    10. Wasn't her first attempt
    11. Broke, no funeral or cremation money
    12. There's a Go Fund Me page
    13. Left a note that read:
      a. *Thanks for leaving me*

III. *Flashback Failed Futuristica*
  A. *I would have got my gun & blew*
  B. *my brains out if I could've just stopped*

32

C. *puking long enough*
>   1. my father said after a 3-day migraine
>   2. I can see
>   3. the blood spattering the curtain
>   4. cacophony of bone & tissue
>   5. washcloth in hand on my hands & knees
>   6. scouring the floor glimpsing gold casing
>   7. under the radiator

D. As if
>   1. the heart alone decides these matters

Love in the Form of Psithurism

       Hadn't I gone
to Speech Therapy
for my extraneous *S, Sh,*
& *Ch* sounds? No love-
lier susurration, like a
phoenix flushed from
the frondescent boscages
of hell, the green soughing
filling the backyard.
The blood clot lodged
in my father's temple
went off like friendly
fire into his brain.
Decades later the flow
of oxygen to my mother's
brain had winnowed
through her clogged
neck arteries from stream
to rill. A slow suffocation
one doesn't notice
until one's slurring,
unable to stick one's
hand into a sleeve—.
I've an anklet of bite
marks from walking
the yard, trying to
transluce the static my
mind is. She's lost
the sewing needle

again. I wave the
magnetic Bingo wand
over where she's been
sitting, stitching.
A pass or few & I
light upon its silver.
What had Krolow
called it?, *playthings*
but of a ghost-
ly nature. *Now—*
now my mother
  remembers where
          the wooden bowls are.

[hurt, —remembering]

hurt,   —remembering
                              is dead."
                                                    "There is no
way to freshen the rotten egg,

                         fire,
                         a cigarette in   my mouth.
whisper   over a final night
stirred

                                        a double ceremony,

                                   a
star,   veil
you…

hurt, —remembering is dead." / "There is no way to freshen/ the rotten egg, / fire, a
cigarette in my mouth. / whisper over a final night/ stirred a double ceremony, / a star veil/ you..

Love in the Form of QVC Binge

And still it snowed. It rained in me[1].
We're still missing the same spools
Of thread as yesterday. My mother eats
From my container of walnuts, sun-
Flower seeds, & craisins. Shuts
The lid. Says *this is good.* Then
Opens the lid
& begins munching again.
Who am I to say
What her hunger is. I've hidden my pot
Pipe on the other side of the deck. Was
Going to pour myself a glass
Of afternoon wine & was
Met with: *isn't it early?*
Who am I to say
What hour it is
Inside my mother?
I would've ordered the robot
Vacuum but not the lazy
Susans. Definitely not
The snap lid travel Tupperware
Like faceless nesting dolls. Bull
In a china shop is how my mother
Enters the back porch door.
Who am I to say how to thunder
Back into life. A bug
Tried to enter my mouth
But I'm tight lipped. So it skimmed
Delineation, brushed upon my chin.

37

Again & again & again she licks
the thread & jams it at the needle's eye, fraying.
I wish my mother was *here*
but who am I to say who this woman is
        within my mother?

---

[1]Brecht

Mercy, for the Connoisseur of Sugar

Give me this day my daily give me this give me this day, my
daily soaked bread, my analgesic, my simple syrup, give me
need, give me grass blade, give me teaspoon, give me weathervane

I crave a little morsel more, dark forest bliss, velvet holiday
Give me, give me a goddamn cigarette I peel back the shade,
take a peek, a lick, I can't hurt from in here—when planets collide

when planets collide there is *this* chthonic green, in the universe
sometimes things go awry—O Lord I'm green, I'm green it's
only my flesh, it's only rotten cake, worm food, a confection suit

Did you say something? I said, did you say something? Don't
leave me, I'm happy as a bowl of batter, did you say something,
what seems to be what what seems to be the matter with you?

Jesuschrist this high's got me by my eyeballs Jesuschrist did you
say something? Patty cake, Patty cake Jesuschrist, I thought I heard
something, one cube or two? Jesuschrist is that me I hear Jesuschrist

is that me, if I die before I wake, oh Butcher oh Baker oh Maker
the sugar cube ran away with the spoon I'm over the moon now give
Give it to me give it give it give it to me I'm the poison eater—*givey*

Elegy for the Dodo

To be known only by description creates a sense of mystery.
In Roelandt Savery's *Landscape with Birds*, among turkey

vultures & parrots, flamingos & ducks, solitaire you, you stare
into water. In the park I Hansel & Gretel your cushat cousins

crushed pretzels & crumbs. O dumb-dumb! O Dodo!
If you knew stranger-danger, if you didn't waddle right up

to the gun! Now behind a pane of museum glass, taxidermied-
you presides beside bone-you. Though it was that girl Alice who

bestowed you widespread attention, affixing you as a symbol
of extinction & obsolescence. Even your disappearance's swaddled

in colossal myth. I, too, have felt myself a creature cloaked
in loss. In the park I scatter popcorn for bobbing, cooing squabs,

some with radar eyes, some with feathers missing. O pigeons
& doves, pigeons & doves! I fall in & out of love, they fall from above.

How Many Fingers Am I Holding Up?

If I don't write you down how will I remember you

In the days of ash-
trays on the nightstand & Skittles
& Stoli for breakfast,

grackles perched
on her collar bones & you could whet
your straight razor on her cheekbones.

If I don't write you down how will I remember you

If I don't write you down

Gorge.
The days she ate just to taste

it coming back up (ice

cream just a warmer version of itself,

& the sicklysweet ketchup she'd drink
from the bottle), &

the days she'd go without.

How will I

How will I

Out of curiosity she ate the pickled octopus.
Tried the thinnest taste of herring
for good luck.
Refused the head–
cheese but jabbed
her fingers in the still-steaming pudding.
She dreamt the burnt cake
but not her burnt spoon
of want. Of the seven deadly sins,
she was Greed. Wore

If I don't write you down

How will I remember you

If I don't write you

her needs on her sleeve.
Tripping on LSD on her way
to a party, she could see colors
behind the colors. When she arrived. When she arrived,
she bugged.

she bugged.
Her mind all spiders in the bananas.

How will I remember

You

Music avalanched from the speakers, ate her
from the inside out.
Her skin didn't fit. Turned slippery.
& her bones, sparrow-

hollow such that she swayed, she drifted.
Samaris & butter-
flies, she couldn't tell the difference
between her thoughts & my voice.

If I don't

If I don't write you

The hall ended abruptly. She made TNT—
that's what he called himself—TNT
bring her home
(which he did) (eventually).

In the days of *The Coliseum*
                she fused on the dance floor,
                                sucked down luminescent shots.

You down how

Picked her wicked stick, blue-tipped
the nipple, lined quarters along the
red felt
of the pool table. Beaming up
in the bathroom. No love
was ever
enough.
Snapping bubble gum,

Will I remember you if

I don't write you

she was lost

Down how will I remember you

If I don't write

even when she never left the
hourly room. Almost over-

dosed

twice—once
by accident, once

by misunderstanding. Cave inside a glacier

                              Down

her sinuses were benumbed by blizzard,
she breathed, breathed, breathed
her mind a whiteout, triggering an avalanche in
the heart's chambers.

                              How

                              Will

The 'shrooms Shelly gave
her, said divide the bag,
sprinkle over takeout.

                    You down how

                Will I remember you if

I don't write you

Down how

These times not
      to be confused
            with when she ended
                  up between worlds
                        in the ER, IV
            affixed into her, its slow drip
      tethering her between.

      In all cases it was a matter
of miscalculation.

Will I remember you

Not like
when she ate the piece of chalk.

Not like when she took the piece of chalk
& bit into it,

thinking: bone of milk; fossil stick; cloud pill.
How it was like a petrified marshmallow, a brittle cake, a core

sample of moon

against her teeth.
How often her

tongue betrayed   her.

I'll remember

you

[quiet. I should be thought; I'd]

quiet. I should be   thought; I'd
make a marvelous acid   .   bit-
ter   .   I
                                        question,
                abundantly clear
the living.
                                look   as if   to
go away.   but instead,
                                wait
        sit   on the bench.
slightly, disliking the awkward
                        nearness.   stay   all af-
ternoon silent,   to speak.
                                ...

                        so Victorian, using such elegant
and inadequate verbs.   light-

experience, being   denounced   I
shall treasure

                        only God   ...
        and

suffering,   show   face.

a long breath like

apology.   I

was

the recipient of his

wanting

thunder damnation and then   vic-
tim . "I was your church,"

quiet. I should be thought;/ I'd make a marvelous acid. / bit-/ ter. I question, abundantly clear
the living. / look as if to go away. / but instead, wait/ sit on the bench. / slightly, disliking the
awkward nearness. / stay all af-/ ternoon silent, / to speak… so Victorian, using/ such elegant
and inadequate verbs. / light-/ experience, being denounced/ I shall treasure only God… and
suffering, / show face. a long breath like apology. / I was the recipient of his wanting/ thunder
/damnation/ and then vic-/tim. "I was your church,"

Love in the Form of "Nip," "Smidgen," "Pinch," & "Dash"

                    Because it's vegan—milk-
              less, egg-less, butter-less—my mother
    & I make Depression
    Cake. Even when hunger's absent, hunger
    is hunger. I smell
    like a goat lost in beardtongue.
    It's ten in the morning &
    I'm sipping Limoncello-
    flavored seltzer. The secret
    ingredient in Tomato Cake (aka Mystery
    Cake) is: tomato. And the recipe for One
    Egg Cake calls for a single egg.
    And yet not an ounce of lightning
    is needed to make Lightning Cake.
    This is also true of Sunshine & Daffodil
    Cakes, albeit they at least
    require the exotic-
    sounding cream of tartar. I'm wearing an apron
    that reads
                    Don't Make Me
                    Poison Your Food.
    When jokingly
    Shane asks if our cake's made of
    real depression I don't have to answer.
    We cut into it. Still dragon-
              breathing from inside. Shovel
                    it with our hands into our pieholes.

Last Supper

"*Nothing ever ends
poetically. It ends and we
turn it into poetry. All that
blood was never once
beautiful. It was just red.*"

—*Blake Volland*

And the tomato sauce
was never once beautiful.
It was just red. I mean
after the wine & the crying
& silences the dinner you
announced you were leaving,
after it clotted, a rim around
the pot I'd have to soak all
the next day, then scour, that
viscera-like residue was a
darker red then, a scabbing.
I wanted to chuck the saucepan
into the street like a *fuck-it*, let
crockery crash like a gong,
give the neighbors something
else to bitch about but it was
my only pot. With a butter
knife I pecked away at the
once hardened, now softening—
what had you called it? oh
that's right—*gravy*.

[a picture of the evening]

a picture   of the   evening

                    to discover
            midnight—
                        gorging   and pre-
tending to take notes.

                        I slid my hand through
                                I
        could smell the musty odor of sweat in an un-
cleaned suit.

                            muttered

                              ...

"I have   questions,"
  my hand   against
another
and gently   'Damned

            under   breath.
                                        I mutt

            "Please

            ?"

52

I murmured sweetly. "What's your name?"
and I didn't come for supper; I
came to   get   alone

a picture of the evening to discover/ midnight gorging/ and pre-/ tending to take/ note. I slid my hand through/ I could smell/ the musty odor of sweat in an un-/ cleaned suit. / muttered... I have questions, / against my hand another/ and 'Damned under breath. / I mutt/ "Please?" I murmur/ sweetly. "What's your name?"/and I didn't come for supper;/ I came to get alone

Do not pity the deer,

rubbing against one another
in the paddock, trying to dodge
the queen's arrows.
They've been collected
for this occasion.
She'll not kill them
all. As another dart is loaded,
lute fiddlers fiddle their lutes &
an imp, dressed in feathers,
garbles a fairy song. Seventy
degree afternoon. The smell of
mud & lavender. Thick trees!
She strikes behind the heart.
The deer juts, circles back
toward the herd, the herd
scatters. *It's like playing marbles!*
one woman exclaims, sipping
from a porcelain cup.
It's like picking flowers! says
a tall man. *It's all a lark!*
says the harpooned doe, falling.
Pity the beasts
not, for what a fine meal
their scraps will make
for the royal hounds! How
ever-lovely the mounted head
as trophy above her Majesty's bed.

[heart]

heart

dragged the bags
into the yard and tried to relock the door

clear
stars
of taxi windows

squint—   needing only
    fingerprint and signature   the
paste dries thoroughly
                          This must *not*

    disturb

                paws   fur and whiskers
    murmured

                    Isn't it a lovely night?
    I must be out of my mind

                    sitting here, letting
you cook up elaborate plots

heart/ dragged the bags/ into the yard/ and tried to relock/ the door/ clear stars of taxi
windows/ squint—fingerprints and signature/ the paste dries thoroughly/ This must *not*
disturb/ paws fur and whiskers/ murmured Isn't it a lovely night? I must be out of my mind/
sitting here, letting you/ cook up elaborate plots

Harlequin Punch & Spider Corn Bread

like ghostsmoke, like basement
quiffe
a soft must rises
as I breathe in the almost century-
year-old pages

here are recipes for Tongue
in Tomato Sauce,
   Roasting Suckling Pig,
     Pigeon Pie,
       Gooseberry Bar-Le-Duc
when serving
eggs on toast to children

or invalids cut
the toast into *small cubes, leaving*
the slice in its original
shape, before putting on the eggs

when darning thinned
stocking-heels, use silk
to *make parallel lines of fine chain stitches*
there're instructions

for making night suits
which sound like
but are not suits
sewn of night's very webbing
this morning

56

after walking the yard
I picked a tick
off my ankle   torched the bloodsucker with a lighter
then asked the sky & grass

for forgiveness   there's a trick
to achieving *a neat, satisfactory buttonhole*
that involves chalk *&* machine

to keep the sink shining-clean?
soap jelly

to convince a child to drink her
milk? try a straw
or a tiny pitcher

but the little ribboned girl in the kitchen refusing
her cup of cow juice has become ragamuffin-

me stuck at the table
            on Augusta Street

staring into a bowl of vomit-

like stew of
      chunked ham,
               pink sauce
                       & macaroni noodle
my drunken grandfather's made

I'll *sit there all goddamn day*
he says if I don't
eat it

Poem Primarily About Moss

No delicacy, no doorway into the phantasmagoric. Simple-
leaved. Flowerless. Diminutive. Most primitive. Cult-
ivated for centuries by Zen Masters as holy gardens. Hair-

cap. Spine-leaf. Hornwort. The 'rice' of the caribou's diet?
Reindeer Moss. Ingredient once kneaded into bread? *Iceland Moss.*
Misnamed lichens. Even the filigree corsages of *Spanish Moss*

pinned in Southern boughs are pineapple-begotten. *Mountain
Pincushion, Glittering Wood,* & *Obtuse Bog-Spiral Extinguisher.*
Bryophytes threatening to occult forest floor & mausoleum alike—

given damp & shadowed conditions. Luminous copper-hungry
copper- & cord moss exposing substrata. O, pioneers cinching fis-
sures between cabin logs as if stuffing a pig's mouth, from under

your caked nails does *rain dew fog sunlight earth* fill your nostrils?
O, mothers of Lapland, lining your babies' cradles with quilts
of azoic growth as if they were nests, like a bassinette left in bulrush,

when you lean in to dust the foreheads of your sleeping ones with
a kiss, do you breathe in the sour milk & chromosomes until
the Hades of your own minds branch inward, whispering deepest losses?

[I explained the peculiar]

I explained the peculiar
telepathy.

Now

I only get impressions.

my feeling was gone—

the message

and the wire
I couldn't think what to do but
pretend to

know

a hole in the ground,

—I learn you've

. . .

disappeared

I explained the peculiar telepathy. / Now I only get impressions. / my feeling was gone—the message/ and the wire/ I couldn't think what to do but pretend to know a hole in the ground/ --I learn you've...disappeared

The Disintegration of Annie

Once upon a timeline, a girl—hypnotized by shapes & sizes—decided
it very best to become thin as a grin. Under this potion, she reverted

to the notion that the world *was* indeed flat. She spat over the horizon
& pointed. *See! Clearly my spittle has utterly disappeared!* Next Annie

changed her name to *I*. *The skinniest letter!* I proclaimed. In the micro-
scopic topic of punctuation, exclamations replaced pesky, robust

questions. In fact, I made a list: marbles were traded for pick-up-sticks;
her puppy for a garden snake; crumb, instead of cake; pin stripe over

hound's tooth; cigarette over pipe; broth replaced stew; broom, vacuum;
cards for dice; needle & thread over loom; silhouette against portrait...

until nothing fit quite right. So teeny-tiny was she, you could count
her ribs one, two, three! It had taken a while but I managed to whittle

herself awfully little. Her bony, tapered fingers gripped her wishbone
hips & she smiled with paper-thin almost gone lips.

Love in the Form of Far-Offness

Although my mother's back yard abuts
The graveyard
I've yet to visit the family plots.
Grandparents. Aunts. Uncles.
My father.

It's going to be dangerous out
Today the newscaster warns.
Where my mother drops
A thing, I pick it up. I chase her
Around the house
The way a mocking
Bird might
Chase after a cat.

Today she asked if I was *trying*

To annoy her.
On a shelf in a closet
Is the only picture of me.

I imagine faking my death. To vanish
Without being erased at the fat heart
Of it.

Not disappearance. Something holier
Like inexactitude & diastole[1].
Something between reckoning & wrecking
Ball.

I call home but no one answers.

---

[1] The phase of the heartbeat when the heart muscle relaxes and allows the chambers to fill with blood

Twyndyllyngs[1]

In the crypt of a dresser drawer faintly wafting of myrrh & Pine-
Sol, I discover the disenvoweled note. Language exposed as a heart

during surgery: a journey in words/a journey inwards. Gypsum
hymn, that afternoon I dedicated myself to defragmentizing your

skeletal nonce, injecting ink nuclei into coda as if fashioning
a ransom note from hieroglyphics. "Th" metastasized into

the, thee & *thou.* Was it *worship* or *warship* you'd intended?
Imprint in print, did "mnstr" mean *ministry, minister* or *monster?*

Was "mnd" *mind, mined, mend, mooned* or *amend?* I was hooked.
Like syzygy[2], you'd strung a string thru the strange. Like a sylph[3]

floating along a statue-lined xyst[4] whilst a lynx wandered the fern-
rich ghyll[5], I was carried away. Of course my alphabet-exorcism-

puzzling-back-together undid whatever mystery your excising did.

So I let be, be. But tell me—was it *levee, levy, lava, live, love, leave*
or *alive* you were insinuating when, at the end, you abbr. "lv" & failed

to flourish your name?

---

[1] (obsolete) a twinling or twin
[2] a conjunction or opposition, especially of the moon with the sun
[3] an imaginary spirit of the air; a mainly dark green and blue hummingbird, the male of which
has a long forked tail
[4] a covered portico, as a promenade; (in an ancient Roman villa) a garden walk planted with
trees
[5] a narrow stream; rivulet; a wooded ravine

["Yes," I said, glancing at my wrist]

"Yes," I said, glancing at my wrist   in a
sliver of light   blind
             wild in love

       and
                    God,
     so cruel   his face
 his hands,   looked the message:

                         o

figure
    a long breath,
  a   fix   a finger
        collapsed
           unstrung
merely   wild and
found   far

"Yes," I said, glancing at my wrist in a sliver of light/ blind wild in love/
and God, / so cruel his face/ his hands, looked the message: o figure/ a
long breath, a fix/ a finger collapsed/ unstrung merely wild and found far

Conjurer

Looking for a razor
under the sink I discover
instead a bottle
of your *Drakkar Noir.*
No cramming the thunder-
head of a genie
back into the thimble
of its lamp—when one spritz
conjugates you & you come back
to me sensually—that is, *of the senses,*
as undertones of mandarin & lemon
juxtaposed with ambiguation's
spiced essence, herbaceous heart closing
on its lavender midnight forest base—Pine
Barrens or Catskills—waft of *Djinn,*
supernatural entity occupying
a parallel world, huffing in *madness,*
scorching fire, smokeless flame—
blood flushes my cheeks
as if I were standing too close
to a guillotine, no, no
unconjuring you now. You slice
through me, gasp & breath, I reel.

[Problems, problems, in every direction: what]

Problems, problems, in every direction: what
to say about   origin

         meant only to entrap me
Most of all, what was the status between

      the kiss

               —and

                              hell   if
we slated for
      the slightest desire

Problems, problems, in every direction: what to say about origin/ meant only to entrap me/ Most of all, what was the status/ between the kiss—and hell/ if we slated for the slightest desire

Elegy of the Tigerwolf[1]

Yours is an afterlife of devil's waltz
strawberries. I meant no trespass.
Close your mouth, open your eyes.
The negative meaning being: throat
of howl & electricity behind
the blindness. A mock sun, a lost cloud.
Babbling wildflowers impale
themselves upon their stalks, frothing
bubbles. I screamed ferns.
From age of moonset, until
around 5:15—when dawn's first streaks
appear in the east—the sky'll be
moodring & darkle. Silence
is the combination of all colors.
It is written: *I am Made perfect thru the blood…*
I cover my doorpost & possessions with the blood…
& *Let me Speak*
the mystery… But what is mystery
& what is blood. Angel wings
& daisies sprout in the vacancies
your footprints have left. *In you*
is all of heaven. When you appeared
after such absence—phantasmagoria,
shadows within shadows—a vision
I could not reckon. What *but* illusion
is heaven? Meaning, here's some jam
for your bread crust—& a smattering
of honeybutter.

---

[1] Tigerwolves, like dodos, are, most unfortunately, extinct.

[relax]

                                        relax
reach   for my hand.

                  Mother   light
     morning   would arrive for
love and   silks
     Silks? "Oh,   the

                  bubbling like
waiting
                            Mother
need   I   thought of
an old-fashioned

                                        I said
light   overcome with   de-
sign and drape   my stitches

                  frame   my room; I always

                  alphabet and numbers—and a frieze
of birds and animals around the edge. I
                                  everything

except the name:
and the date,   Those stitches
after all,
may be forgiven,
squeeze my hand again, "Now tell me

relax/ reach for my hand. / Mother light/ morning would arrive for love and silks/ *Silks?* "Oh, bubbling like waiting/ Mother need/ I thought of an old-fashioned/ I said light overcome with de-/ sign and drape my stitches/ frame my room; I always alphabet/ and numbers—and a frieze/ of birds and animals/ around the edge. / I everything except the name:/ and the date, Those stitches/ after all, may be forgiven, / squeeze my hand again, / "Now tell me

Love in the Form of Rock-a-Bye Baby

I threw up my vegetable soup
Dinner. Too much sun–
In-a-cup at Turtle's pool
The day before I guess. Severe
Thunderstorm warning in effect.
Around five the darkening, the cat
Meowing at the glass door. She's
Still there this morning
Pacing the porch, mewing
As I drink coffee, eat a sweet
Potato smothered in lentils.
I wish I had some Jamaican Curry
Spice but I've nutritional yeast.
If I had a piece of chicken I'd
Feed her that—the stray—even though
Frank said, *don't feed that cat;*
Don't feed that cat I'll never
Get rid of it. My mother picked
Up my journal—to read it
& I took it from her, *you can't read*
That I said & she replied
Not un-sarcastically *I didn't*
Know it was your innermost
Thoughts. What do you think
I write then, I stunned. Green shoots
Spear through the mulch
In the flowerpot on my mother's
Railing: wildflower seeds
I dumped in there two weeks

Ago just to see if they'd take
Purchase. The splinters of marigold
Seeds still atop the leaf litter.
Below my window last night
The human-like yowling, the forest
Of the yard swishing in the stirred
Weather, my head hot my body
Chilled, my own trembling toward
Sleep—of course birds are linked
To one's sense of happiness; it's to do
With the nests & the having
Materialized out of an egg, & perhaps
The bit about ascent, &
                    Descending through air.

What the Scapegoat Whispered

Sacred geometry. I was afraid
my face was me.
Then I feared it wasn't.
Meanwhile grass continued growing
out of my chest
as if I were already a grave.
Meanwhile my smeary reflection inverted
in the brass doorknob
looked like melting.
I'm exposed not because
I'm naked
but because I'm multidimensional
& diamond-eyed.
Cold knob warned, *You are living*
in a dangerous world & cannot speak in flora.
And the cold brass
of a bell cried, *I cannot tell*
my innermost self
from my outermost self
& my emptiness has its own sound.

Sound curls in the tunnel of my ear

Picking at the split ends
Or lighting matches
Just to blow them
Out I could
Distance myself
From myself
The first time I
Came I thought I
Pissed myself
My hands cramped
Into lobster
Claws
My tongue furred
Mouth went dry
He shut
The door
Behind him
Left me leaning
Against the vanity
Beside the shower
Curtain
Wiping
My nose
The inner side
Of my thigh with a tissue
The desire
To want
To kill
Oneself

Differs
From
The desire
To want
To die
One being
Where river spills
The other being
The spilling
I didn't want
To die
I wanted
Never
To have
Been born
To not have quickened
But now
That I'm here
Is it the death or the dying
I fear? I mean—one can't feel
One's own absence can one?

[the doorway of]

           the doorway   of
       chiseled   gold
waves, shadowed eyes and

                                                 even
       stream   —   I was lighting a cig-
arette   (who asked to be called
)—
                                                 I knew I was
facing the firing squad.
       I'd been able to turn so I never faced
directly; could I   catch my
breath,
                       I'm *hagged*—I need a dab of powder
…
                                                       to
diehard and in a ringing voice,
                I   forget—   waiting at
the door

the doorway of chiseled gold waves/ shadowed eyes/ and even stream—I was lighting a ciga-
rette (who/ asked to be called)—I knew I was/ facing the firing squad. / I'd been able to turn/
so I never faced directly;/ could I catch/ my breath, I'm *hagged*—I need a dab/ of pow er…/
to diehard and in a ringing voice, / I forget—waiting at the door

Fish in the Bougainvillea

       As if blue sky were a glass tank
of sea & the punches
of fuchsia were sprays
of coral reef & not papery
valentines who, in coming days,
will litter the sidewalk—what sunken kingdom dreams
       do you think that that fish,
like a fixed weather-
vane atop the gate—would drum up
in its icy brain

if it weren't frozen
in art? Would it imagine itself
a copper swimmer
tangled in the net
of fiery bougainvillea, a fish in a tree?

Maybe stir-crazy as any
below-the-surface-
creature, thoughts of salt—*the air
thick with it*—would brine its prehistoric mind?

       Or would something
of the umbrella
of shadow it idles beneath
fascinate it dizzy
until it broke loose, hungry
for the clouds? But a flying fish's

a stranger idea
than an ancestor
hiding in a climbing-bush.
I mean, from when
        we were of the waters.

        Before our invention
of fire. & song.
& bicycle.
A blue one. With a basket & a bell.
This bike. The one I'm riding,
Neptune charioting
a dolphin, down this sunny lane with its ginger-
bread trimmed shotgun
houses & mermaid
mailboxes & the slightly-open
mouthed, welded fish.

        I on my way & it on its,
like future & past journeying
in different directions
& still nevertheless
crossing paths.

[I burrowing weeping]

I   burrowing   weeping
from combined nerve strain and loving

                                bodily
      gently wiping   I
ruined those beautiful eyes,   softly
                  lovely
elegantly,   —but it turns *your*   green
      sweetheart calm and   serious
         —vanished
I lay silent, distracted thinking

          cigarette lighted
        —and I still don't know what to say.

                              Am I
merely ego

I burrowing, weeping—from combined nerve, strain/ & loving bodily—
gently I ruin those beautiful eyes, / softly, lovely, elegantly—but it turns
your green/ sweetheart calm & serious—vanished I lay silent, / distracted
thinking, cigarette lighted—and still/ don't know what to say. Am I merely ego? /

Recap in Nonlinear Time

What did the one barfly say to the other?
Here, I saved this stool for you!

Joke, Author Unknown

Vanessa asked when
I was little what did
I want to be, a scientist?
Because of the scientific
language, the nature
imagery. No, an astronaut.
A ballerina. But I was
told I was too fat, I said.
This was before we watched
the semblance of a drunken
poet on a screen in a bar.
This was as we ate popcorn
out of paper bowls. And no
one went out for a cigarette
break. And I had glued fake
flies to plastic cups. Because
I was going for theme. I was
setting a mood, a tone. And
Vanessa & her friend cackled
& hooted & roared & cheered
& spilled a drink. And some
people left before the movie
began & some before it ended.

I brought a duffel-bag-sized-bag
of chemically butter-flavored
popcorn home, & the canister
of beer nuts. My cache of poems.
Burning in Water, Drowning
in Flames, fringed in bright
plastic tabs to mark the pages.
The room was bluelit. A dozen
of us had gathered. Then two
men who strayed in from
the streets sat at the bar
unsure if they were welcomed
but weren't turned away so.
I'd forgotten that movie,[1]
Carolyn said. They're so good
together. Who? Fay & Mickey?
No. The poet & the bottle.

---

[1] *BarFly*

[...alone in the world... wake]

...alone in   the   world ...   wake
up,
        full dark.   The mask
loosened while I slept.
                                            I
peered at my wrist, and remembered

                            I could see flood-
    springing up about the   rip.
                            I scarcely felt
contact,
face   to the ground.

                                            who
served him   ? I
place   my hands   down—

                    I never break   —and
                    I'm dying
        —and   mustn't
                      wander   broadly
        my hand
    rushed forward,
                    to be replaced by

                              curves and woodlands
    until at last   I *saw*

    It loomed, it beetled

...alone in the wake/ The mask loosened/ I peered at my wrist, / and could see flood-/ springing up about the rip. / I scarcely felt contact, / face to the ground. / who served him? I place my hands/ down—I never break—and/ I'm dying—and and broadly my hand rushed forward, / to be replaced by curves and woodlands/ until at last I *saw*/ It loomed, i beetled

What Happened to Nancy?

When Danielle tags me in the Facebook post, it's because
someone remembered I bussed dirty plates
at *The Old Country Buffet*. It takes my breath away,

how familiar Nancy looks, like I know her or I should
know her. 20 years & still her murder's unsolved. Blunt
force trauma, Nancy 17 years young at the time, walking

home (? —I'd have to reread the feed). She looks
ghostly-familiar but the story isn't. *Do I
have any information?* the post wonders. And I wish

I did. I study her picture until I think I see her
in the halls at school, tucking her books
into her locker, or behind the cash register

taking customers' money. I don't remember her
being dead—not on the news, on the local TV,
in the stalls of the girls' bathroom, at that dive

restaurant. You'd think a person might remember
a girl she went to school with, maybe worked with,
turning up dead. Maybe I did see her image

on the television or in the newspaper all those years
ago. But the timeline doesn't quite add up. I mean
for our paths to have crossed. I worked at the buffet

on weekends but was fired—no, not fired, *Terminated*
for total insubordination—the Friday before Father's
Day (before graduating college in '99). I know

it was before Father's Day because even after they told
me I was canned, blue apron smudged with biscuit
& gravy sauce, I asked if they wanted me

to work since the restaurant would be busy
& they, stunned as if I perhaps didn't know
what the word *terminated* meant, shook their heads *No...*

Was I dating Dom, or back with A—?
I don't remember a Daniel in the kitchen, I tell Dee;
but I knew a Pete. I don't mention Jill. I don't mention

Jill because. Because she had to save herself & her kids
from her husband. And I, whom famously never remembers
anything, how can I know Nancy's face? How can I ever

not know her face now? I think I see Nancy
walking home. I think if I write about her
I'll remember; or if not me, maybe someone else might?

I remember the name tags we pinned to the navy shirts
we wore; how the grease of fried chicken,
the pucker of sour milk, the glue of syrup

& the bucket-smell of green beans clung into
the weave of that unbreathable fabric. I didn't mean
to write *unbreathable* but I did. I did not mean to write

unbreathable & leave Nancy there on the sidewalk
of this poem as someone left her in the wooded area
behind the Mini Mall in her purple Arizona jacket

& flared light blue jeans, dark V-neck sweater
& black & white platform shoes, her purple
backpack near her, staring lost-like into the trees or dirt

or both, in that cold night, that icy growing icier,
wide growing wider, vacant growing agape, night.

[but in the end,]

but in the end,
what becomes of

you

—

night?

but in the end, what becomes of you—night?

Doppler

Inching in hurricane evacuation traffic—*The greatest mass
exodus in modern history!*—says the news but it troubles me,

the sensationalized language as if this, 'the entire' quagmire
peninsula that is the Sunshine State funneling into other

swelters, was comparable to bloodied displacements, to dis-
locations engendered by wars soaked in the name of

higher power—*The greatest mass exodus in modern history!*
says the news of the line for gas, six vehicles deep, officers

patrolling the pumps, semiautomatics slung over shoulders,
one flicking a cigarette past the two potbelly pigs grunting

in the back of the Jeep beside us as our caravan creeps up
to the petrol nozzle where, surrounded by the things I'd hope

to safe-keep, I stare at the back of a camper proclaiming *Life is Good
But Eternal Life/ Is Better*—as if heaven were perpetual perfect weather,

a total lack of helter-skelter, lemonade, gates of glitter, a magical
shelter. Insurance companies won't cover *Acts of God.* When we

return weeks later, branches bar the door but no windows broken.
Others will have to prove the wind damage was wrought by wind,

the flood damage ravaged by the wrath of water. Tell me, if one
can't prove God's existence how does one prove God's intentional?

[be mutton]

be mutton

dressed as lamb on me. *Promise* you r mind

glass in hand,

and again I felt bewilder-

ment,

Pure chance I came straight on,

and

was *thunderstruck—*

be mutton dressed as lamb on me. / *Promise* you r mind/ glass in hand, / and again I felt bewilder-/ ment, Pure chance/ I came straight/ on, and was *thunderstruck—*

In a Roman Plaza

         Not veiled
in rain, the hills
& churches *sun-*
dressed, such that
even the shadows
were golden.
There are rooms
reserved for prayer.
And rooms lit
only by candle.
Nougat, braided breads,
cured meats displayed
in windows.
In a blush rose,
like a candy wrapper,
a brilliant green
beetle rummaging
the petals while deeper
in the folds bides
a spider. A woman
in pink flip-flops
on the floor outside
the temple door;
then, visiting
one by one
the cafe tables,
asking for alms.
An old man
rooting through his bag

while his wife
looks into the distance.

Love in the Form of Shell Shock

To be inside the un-
Hatched egg, feeling
Along the lining
Of the round ceiling
B(l)ending like a skull,
Body into walls,
Hand spreading
So the fingers
Cast shadows.
I do not know
What goes on
Inside my mother. I sip
A diet soda on the plane
To settle
My stomach. It's claustrophobic
& dreamy inside
The hallow. Bolts
Of silken linen, a candelabra,
Some gangrene plums
On a table.
Samantha blinks
Her eyes when adding
The cards
In Scopa. Danielle en-
Dearingly calls her
The Child. And *Crotch-*
Fruit. My mother suffered
A stroke but it's my thinking

That's been rearranged,
Shuffled, twitching.
Transplant may or may not
Mean what you think it means,
I quoted of my own poem
Last night but why
I can't remember.
Blue-eyed: as in when the snake
Sheds its skin & the trans-
Parent cells veil the head.
You didn't
Think I meant
A bird's egg,
Did you? No, not of
A feathered
Beginning. I meant
Being made anew
On the ground crawling
On my belly,
Sun warming my un-
              Winged back.

Geolocation

How would you describe something so obvious it doesn't
        require further explanation? They are bringing the mother
                to the iced-grass mansion she's occasionally dreamt

about. Out to pasture isn't what was meant but the phrase
        has nevertheless insinuated itself *into*, just as the trajectories
                of Mars & Jupiter, if patterned with string, weave a circle

within a star within a circle suggesting a galactic doily back-
        drop dung beetles compass by. The mother, figure-like
                is being brought. Now by a hairsbreadth the narrative

unhinges, blued at the edges. The maternal is velvet
        unfolding. *Awakening* being the point of view of the burnt-
                orange lampshade in the old parlor; not the shade itself,

but from below the drum's frilled mouth spilling umbra.
        For light too is a form of communication. As echo or
                refraction, as seaglass or extinct(ion), of the endless ways

to be in this world. Somewhere a way refused to emerge
        or was refused. And so became a way of unbeing. Because
                a 'mirage' encysts the 'real object' & the object itself

insists its (own) unstable image, on their way, they looked at—then
        upon—the apex hills. As a puddle acting as a mirror the 'iced-
                grass effect' was the result of the silvery underside

of the sinuate leaf margins; the mansion the consequence of blood
& wonder. Elsewhere, cobwebby soft entangled hairs.
Sometimes what answers, answers from elsewhere
They are bringing the mother.

Love in the Form of Medium (as Vessel)

'All the bells of heaven made
to ring' isn't the same thing as 'being
touched in the head' though
both speak of certain
sensory parts of the brain
being manipulated.
And yet it's said it feels
nothing, that organ
of consideration & function.
"Whatever is received
is received according
to the nature
of the recipient,"
& the spirit of the staircase
looks over its shoulder
but what commands
your attention? I'm washing
my mother's back,
she's rinsing
the bruised incision
between her breasts. She says aloud
"I don't know what I'd do
without you here" but I'm other-
worldly, fey, unheeding, distrait, with-
drawn even as I'm soaping away
the glue matting her hair to her neck
just below her ear.

[I left, never dreaming]

I   left, never dreaming
my letter   lost.
I   was   trying to reach you
                slowly.

                                                    I
        was   asking you to
                              understand   and
then we were cut off.

                                                I don't
understand what became of my letter.
    it was not found   present

    Curiouser and curiouser, because there was no
              I

Considering you're disappointed in me

              because

              I had the impression you
              find   your

97

Clear anger, an incredible deep
sapphire blue

I left, never dreaming/ my letter lost. / I was trying to reach you slowly. / I was ask-
ing you to understand/ and then we were cut/ off. I don't understand what became of
my letter. /--i was not found present/ Curiouser and curiouser, because there was no I/
Considering/ you're disappointed in me/ because I had the impression you find your Clear
anger, / an incredible deep sapphire blue

Because to Dress Means to Eviscerate

The gate hinge makes a frayed nerve sound, opening.
      A bee sound. As if slugs riddled the hive.

Weekly circulars & car wash coupons jut
      from the mailbox, & my father still receiving

Field & Stream Magazine though he's been long gone.
      I've returned to haul bags of what cannot be salvaged

out of the basement & into the garbage.
      My father glossing rib & muzzle, stock wedged

against his thigh, cup of coffee beside him, cigarette
      balanced on the table's edge, smoldering. What

to do with the quiver of arrows denuded
      of their razor tips? Mossy box of brass shells?

The engraved Spey, Sheepfoot & Coping knives?
      What to do with the small chest with its bright

polishing rag & can of oil, its rods & brush?
      Piece of hair in my mouth. Sweat prickling

between my breasts, grime along the inside my arm,
      dirt falls into my glass of water, I drink it anyway,

I drink it because I'm thirsty & the gate is a deer
      strung-up by its hind legs from a tree, twisting

& leaking into a bucket & there's no more ice
     in the ice tray & siren after siren whizzes by & I

I just walked back down those narrow, cluttered
     stairs & it's quiet here. It's quiet. The outside world

muffled beneath this fur-lined Deerstalker cap
     & though I'm sure it'll give me a rash, irritating

my scalp & ears, itching & stinking as if it's been dredged
     from the bottom of a bog & pissed on—mouse

or squirrel or musk—engulfed as I am in its wooly
     silence—a silence one practices, the heart the target—

crouched in cold, one good eye, one bad, one shut, one
     unblinking, as branch becomes antler & antler becomes

the sweet-spot between ribs my father misses
     or doesn't—I can't bring myself to take off this rotten hat.

Is this what it is to be gutted? Emptiness, a body.
     I slip a bullet into my pocket. At the sink I wash my hands

for the umpteenth time. In fact, every time I enter the kitchen
     I scrub my hands. They're still damp when I try the door

to the gun cabinet but that key's been missing
     since I don't remember when.

[I entirely real, and]

I   entirely real,   and

                in such a   mood,

ask

                         the   cup on
the tray   "Mother, forgive me
                          tonight?"

       and

           and I
   gazing at the fire, absorbed in   individual
thought,   remove
         a cigarette
                      to
light
             now,   tell
me what really happened

    I was   a   horsewoman.
    faded blue eyes   compelling
        the horse bolt

---

*I entirely real, / and in such a mood, / ask the cup on the tray/ "Mother, forgive me tonight?" /
and and I gazing at the fire, absorbed/ in individual thought, / remove a cigarette to light/ now,
tell me what really happened/ I was a horsewoman/ faded blue eyes compelling/ the horse bolt*

Ministry

Not you but my mindfeast of you, the phantom image of you
enough—enough for my pores to *zzzzz* with paresthesia,
to thunderstrike & render me bereft as glaciers halv-
ing. *Render:* misted votive; to surrender, as the wick does.
Alone: letters flanking a sigh—0—on an empty, lean lane.
This mind you now dominate, your fingertips stripping a grape-
fruit, grapefruit oil dissipating from your silhouette into
gold air. *Echo:* worship at an invisible temple's door.
As in, I revisit this vacancy crushed by the sublime.
Sublime: also, revise. To oblige is to bind: the leaf mis-
taken for wing the spider forces its silk around, is bound.
Is, too, boundary. Triggerer of affairs dreamt: *you.* Promise—
the vastness, sublimation, when I reenter the room, strick-
en as a bell, I'll be fed by lambent image—acolyte,
in the serving room, the cold-lit *yes* the brass bed made of not.

ars poetica apologia

• • •

The tiger lilies
of my mother's god-

speed-recovery
      bouquet

Do all but inundate[1]

along their petal edges,

shedding selves

• • •

"It's amazing," observes the advertisement for *Alabaster
Bibles*, "how a simple design change can open
people up to experience God in new ways."

• • •

Twin Blooms on a single green stick,
what is the distinction between im-

possible & possible?

I, between thoughts

• • •

meat & sponge

sunshine & murder

paradox & glitter

a ghost dwells in my mind & chops wood in my heart

• • •

Where God is
Satan is

a shadow a
Pleasure

January, all collarbone dressed in leather
a machine's mercuric dream about spires

• • •

A Cup of fog: A Cup of fog.
You could argue I'm claiming *possible* &

impossible to be interchangeable & you

would not be wrong. You would
not be correct either, though.

The breath passing from mouth to ear.

One degree colder & the chance
for snow. Subtext is

to moon containment of spirit as turnip is to beet

• • •

Moon Haiku

How can I survive?
I dreamt the dead were alive.
Vacant gouged city.

• • •

To my surprise
it was the birds & not the chip-
munks & squirrels thieving the sunflower seeds.
This is (like) the line struck

[in revision] from the poem. What is left
of it in the air, in the memory of the place—*neither created nor*
uncreated

(hook, page, datum, quietude) *I wasn't looking back, I was*

• • •

remembering back,
says the toehead in the black&white movie "The Rifleman"

• • •
• • •

The double "u" of vacuum's
always intrigued me—it's evidence

of the impossible. The you
in "u", the double you, the multiplicity of you, the self as a you.

The all vowels
of You. The vows, the end of the alphabet

of those vowels. Y functioning as
a consonant a function
& of course a question, abbreviation, a (dis)solving
as dusk into other light.

Sometimes only the poem knows
to whom to what it's speaking.

• • •

Strand wrote "I feel that anything is possible in a poem"

but CD Wright wrote "it is a poem if I say it is."

• • •
• • •

Echo is residual
sound. Is fragment.

The intangible equivalent
of: a scan.

I never come (to a poem) without
[wanting] (something).

"A lock

upon the heart" an article calls pride,

citing Proverbs.

• • •

To be pro-verb it to be animate, to in-
fuse energy, exchange.
To be pro-noun is to serve the thing.
To be pronounced is a machine live-

transcribing "etymologically" as "Adam
illogically."

• • •

Idolization-> Objectification-> Concentration ->
Quiddity

&
Tangent

(that a stone bridge differ from a stony bridge
differ from stone broke)

• • •

It's wearing me thin.

It's wearing me thin—grief & dirt; horsethief & rust;
the stripping down of belief; the *sudden intervention
of God's saving grace⁴*. The only flowers left "thriving"

are a few milk-colored carnations;
the roses bow, softened hot grimaces.
Something dragon-

like about their curled edges, but I can't quite
define what—æromancy, or how forgiveness
wormwoods the soul... Honeyed-dust, like the damned

looking into paradise, hallucination of heaven:
Gypsophila²—sprigs of baby's
breath—those underrated astral coronets,
suffumigation³, velvet notes

• • •

I need lean in to catch deepened whiff
of--. Something myth-like, wombish, about

the arrangement, its blushful sear.

• • •

The incision
on my mother's
neck begins

below her earlobe
& continues
under her chin.

Dried blood's
crusted some
of the stitches

& pooled blood's
created bruising
along her throat

like strangulation's
sidereal punctuation.
The doctors say

my mother's scars,
when healed, will
hardly be noticeable.

• • •

• • •

• • •

---

[1] Dickinson—poem #137 as found in The Laurel Poetry Series: Emily Dickinson, © 1960
[2] *Of the carnation tribe; cup-like calyx of white-edged green sepals containing five petals in shades of white or pink; contains several kidney- or snail-shell-shaped brown or black seeds; possess detergent qualities; may be used in the production of photographic film, hemolytic laboratory reagents, liqueur, cheese, ice cream, sweet halva; aka 'gyp', 'soap root', 'chalk plant'; also slightly poisonous*—Wikipedia
[3] Magical incense (Daniel Schulke's *Veneficium*)
[4] Online dictionary

Love in the Form of Flowers Drowning Flowers

In Ireland it's a soft day
My mother says of the rain.
Then, *where's my tea cup?*
The devastation & the human,
The animal & the raw.
I have to take my pills
My mother says, taking her pills.
I need clear tape to secure
The book's broken spine,
Cracked & split from holding
It open long enough to tease
Out poems in the form
Of erasures. Making something
Of what's left behind,
What's made missing.
Part of poetry's tragic knowledge,
Michael Palmer writes
Of Carolyn Forché's
"In the Lateness of the World,"
Is that elegy is endless. I write
"I had to come up for air—
What can I say about these poems
But they are cruelly beautiful
Or beautifully cruel? So
Incising, so deft, so (s)tilled."
My mother stretches her neck,
Reaches for, but does not touch,
Her sutures. And I've still yet to visit
My father's grave.

[unconnected]

unconnected

apparently

                                        they

don't know a thing,

self? It *could* still fit—a quick try at getting   off

              I was walking

a   question   answered   of

the inner stairs.   boots

    opened   fire   " joy

                   in the

      slow   path.

       like a giant snowball, there was a

choice of paths. I settled for one that led over a rise,

and could see

        a man

                who doubled as

 a   mast

  I hastened forward,

     I'm not *very*   , am I?"

unconnected apparently they don't know a thing, / self? It *could* still fit—a quick try/ at getting off/ I was *walking*/ a question answered of the inner stairs. / boots opened fire/ "joy in the slow path. / like a giant snowball, there was a choice of paths. / I settled for one/ that led over a rise, / and could see a man who doubled as a mast/ I hastened forward, / I'm not *very,* am I?

Erasure Erasure

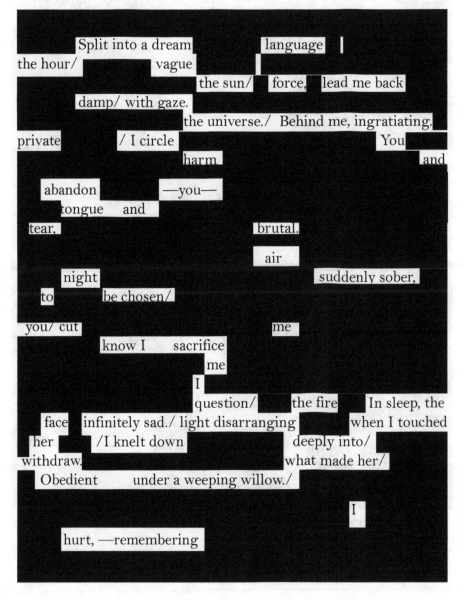

Split into a dream   language   I
the hour/   vague
                the sun/   force,   lead me back
        damp/ with gaze.
                the universe./ Behind me, ingratiating.
private   / I circle   You
                harm   and

    abandon   —you—
        tongue   and
tear,   brutal.

                        air

    night   suddenly sober,
to   be chosen/

you/ cut   me

        know I   sacrifice
                    me
                I
                question/   the fire   In sleep, the
    face   infinitely sad./ light disarranging   when I touched
her   /I knelt down   deeply into/
withdraw.   what made her/
    Obedient   under a weeping willow./

                                        I

    hurt, —remembering

a   star veil/ you..

quiet   slightly, disliking the

awkward nearness./

being   God… and

suffering,/   a long breath like   thunder

I was your church

of sweat   against

breath./

I didn't come   to get   dragged

out of my mind   you/

go —

you   disappear   a sliver of light/ blind wild

love/ and God,/ so cruel   : o   / long breath, a

fix/ a finger   / unstrung   and

what   about

hell/

overcome

around the edge./ I   after all, may be

forgiven,/

—I knew I was/

to die   in a ringing voice,/   —

waiting   weeping—   nerve,   &   bodily

ruin   i

vanished I lay

lamb   wild   -/

/ I   was   alone in the wake/ The

flood

replaced curves and woodlands/
I was trying to
reach you slowly./ I was asking you to understand/

an incredible deep sapphire blue

fire,

I was   /
unconnected
I was walking   the inner
stairs.

as a mast/

Split into a dream language/ the hour vague/ the sun force lead me back, / damp with gaze. / the universe. Behind me, ingratiating/ private/ I circle You/ harm and abandon— you—/ tongue and tear,/ brutal air/ night suddenly sober,/ to: be chosen/ you cut me/ know I sacrifice me/ I question the fire In sleep, the face infinitely sad./ light disarranging/ when I touched her I knelt down deeply into withdraw./ what made her Obedient/ under a weeping willow./ I hurt, —remembering a star veil/ you quiet slightly/ disliking the awkward nearness/ being God…and suffering,/ a long breath like thunder/ I was your church/ of sweat/ against breath./ I didn't come to get dragged out of my mind/ you go—/ you …disappear a sliver of light/ blind wild love and God,/ so cruel:/ o long breath, a fix/ a finger unstrung/ and what about hell overcome/ around the edge./ I after all, may be forgiven,/ —I knew I was to die in a ringing/ voice/ waiting, weeping—nerve and bodily ruin/ i vanished I lay lamb wild/ I was alone in the wake/ The flood replaced curves and woodlands/ I was trying to reach you slowly/ I was asking you to understand an incredible deep sapphire blue fire,/ I was unconnected/ I was walking the inner stairs/ as a mast

114

Collect Call from Outer Space—Do You Accept the Charges?

Was it the body or mind
which was more un-
kind? Despite embalmed
sleep, crackling in their dark-
emporium, the hair & nails continued
elongating into hexagonal
butterflies, the scaffolding of shadows.
Or the skin simply shrank back.
These instincts
I try to find vocabulary
for. I sat by the statue
& was mistaken for statue
so still I stayed. Still, as in
apparatus used for distilling liquids
as well as becalmed. The grand illusion
that any of us could be
saved. Though,
there were reasons to want
to believe. The cave wall's char-stain
was mistaken for a three-headed god. No,
the charcoal rubbings
of eroded gravestones
that hung on the gallery's
slick white walls, too expensive to look at,
beladened I mean deadened
god in me. Bughouse
is another word for funny
farm, insane asylum, bedlam, laughing

academy, booby hatch, nut
house, loony bin, madhouse,
rubber room, sanatorium, snake pit, psych
ward, & in South Amboy:
fourth floor. Maud said
Writing makes a shape
of silence so I began arranging
myriagons of pressed lips,
isotopes of whisperings. In another dimension
you are writing this to me.
In another's dream, I am
the impossible sempiternal touch, the rain
carving ribs into the cave, the cave
growing teeth. In a different hour
you & I never cross paths.
Or we cross paths, only one through the other
like a knife through
an echo. Found on oozins.tumblr:

JESSICA HAS A
FOREHEAD SCAR
FROM THE DEEP
END OF A POOL

I ASK JESSICA WHAT
DROWNING FEELS LIKE
AND SHE SAYS
NOT EVERYTHING FEELS
LIKE SOMETHING ELSE

To say
I've made my life of hair & nail
is to affirm I've tended
to the body. Changing
a cage into a boat is a gesture
towards salvation. You can daydream
about killing yourself
without wanting
to swallow
razorblades. I've wanted to
wake up after a nap
or stint in one of those
sensory deprivation chambers
& feel re-born-into, to
hear my thoughts & blood pulsing.
When I etched the scar & stitches
on my wrist in pen it was
for the sake of
the vision. When I
read "quantum
mechanics views sub-
atomic particles as 'tendencies
to exist,'" I misread it as *tenderness*
& was, thereafter.

Acknowledgements

Many thanks to the editors of the follwing journals for publishing these poems, sometimes in slightly differnet incarnations

Crab Creek Review: "Static," "Fourth Floor Ward"

Guesthouse: "Some Scratch About Aesthetics," "Aesth, Scratch, Cont"

Jai Alai: "Ministry"

Menacing Hedge: "Geolocation" "Elegy of the Tigerwolf"

Oberon: "The Disintegration of Annie"

Red-Headed Stepchild: "The Connoisseur of Sugar"

Serving House Journal: "Decapitation"

Whiskey Tit: "Graveyard Squall"

ZYZZYVA: "Recap in Nonlinear Time"

"In a Roman Plaza" appeared in a micro-anthology handmade by Tracey Knapp which evolved out of attending La *Romita* Writing Conference.

Erasures culled from pulp goth novel "Dark Moon, Lost Lady" by Elsie Lee

According to Ware's Victorian Dictionary of Slang and Phrase, "a sentimental hairpin" is "an affected, insignificant girl."

On August 31, 2021, "a Barnegat man [was] arrested and charged with the 1999 slaying [of Nancy Noga.]" The killer has been "indicted on first-degree murder, first-degree felony murder, first-degree aggravated sexual assault, first-degree kidnapping and third-degree possession of a weapon for an unlawful purpose in the killing of 17-year-old Nancy Noga."

I'd like to acknowledge the writing conferences and/or organizations which have supported my writing: The National Endowment of the Arts; Bread Loaf Writers' Conference; Sewanee Writer's Conference; Tin House Writers' Conference; Squaw Valley Writers' Community; Napa Writer's Conference; The Studios of Key West; Key West Literary Seminar; Winter Poetry and Prose Getaway; Key West Poetry Guild; La Romita.

This manuscript would not be possible without the support of my dear friends and mentors, including but not limited to: Kim Addonizio; JD Adler; Elizabeth Agans; Kazim Ali; Lisa Ampleman; Renee Ashley; Rick Barot; Steve Bellin-Oka; Gabrielle Calvocoressi; Noreen Cargill; Belo Miguel Cipriani; Kalo Clarke; Lance Cleland; Michael Collier; Billy Collins; Lisa Fey Coutley; Julia Kolchinsky Dasbach; Natalie Diaz; Risa Denenberg; Ellen Devin; Cat Doty; Stephen Dunn; Vievee Francis; Daisy Fried; Forrest Gander; Amber Gilewski; Christine Gosnay; Kathleen Graber; Linda Gregerson; Jennifer Grotz; Kelly Boyker Guillemette; Courtney Harler; Kenneth Hart; Arlo Haskell; Bob Hass; Brenda Hillman; Edward Hirsch; Sally Keith; Tracey Knapp; Jason Lamb; Susan Landgraf; Timothy Lindner; Katharyn Howd Machan; Dawn Manning; Laura McCullough; Mary Meriam; Lauren Monahan; Peter Murphy; Matthew Olzmann; Gregory Pardlo; Tod Perry; Carl Philips; Paul Reubens; David Rivard; Mary Ruefle; Leila Rupp; James Russel; Mary Jo Salter; Brenda Shaughnessy; Evie Shockley; Tom Sleigh; Betsey Marks Smith; Donna Noodle Spruijt-Metz; A. E. Stallings; Lauren Stella; Mark Strand; Mary Szybist; Verta Taylor; Adam Vines; BJ Ward; Richard Weems; Ross White; Arida Wright; Kevin Young.

Special thank you to the amazing jackalopes at Tolsun, especially Risa Pappas, Heather Lang, Bridgette Brados, and David Pischke for all their patience, encouragement and support.

Hearts to my family. Lots of love to Mumzee. And my brother Shane, with whom I share a brain.

Extra love to Vicki.

And if you don't see your name here, forgive me and please know I love you, too.

LGBTQ+ writer and former Key West Poet Laureate, Flower
Conroy is the author of the chapbooks *Facts About Snakes &*
Hearts, *The Awful Suicidal Swans*, and *Escape to Nowhere*. Her first
full-length manuscript, *Snake Breaking Medusa Disorder* was chosen
as the winner of the NFSPS Stevens Manuscript Competition.
Her poetry has appeared in *New England Review*, *Prairie Schooner*,
Michigan Quarterly Review, *American Literary Review* and other journals.

CPSIA information can be obtained
at www.ICGtesting.com
Printed in the USA
FSHW011208121121
86157FS